W9-CSO-816

EXTREME JOBS IN EXTREME PLACES

LIFE ON A
COMMERCIAL
FISHING BOAT

By Oscar Sylvester

Gareth Stevens
Publishing

Please visit our website, www.garethstevens.com. For a free color catalog of all our high-quality books, call toll free 1-800-542-2595 or fax 1-877-542-2596.

Library of Congress Cataloging-in-Publication Data

Sylvester, Oscar.
 Life on a commercial fishing boat / Oscar Sylvester.
     p. cm. — (Extreme jobs in extreme places)
 Includes index.
 ISBN 978-1-4339-8488-4 (pbk.)
 ISBN 978-1-4339-8489-1 (6-pack)
 ISBN 978-1-4339-8487-7 (library binding)
 1. Fisheries—Juvenile literature. 2. Fishers—Juvenile literature. I. Title.
 SH331.15.S95 2013
 639.2—dc23

                              2012022061

First Edition

Published in 2013 by
Gareth Stevens Publishing
111 East 14th Street, Suite 349
New York, NY 10003

Copyright © 2013 Gareth Stevens Publishing

Designer: Andrea Davison-Bartolotta
Editor: Therese M. Shea

Photo credits: Cover, pp. 1, 24, 25 Natalie Fobes/Stone/Getty Images; pp. 4, 11 courtesy of NOAA photo library; pp. 5, 13 Dan Rafla/Aurora/Getty Images; p. 6 Hemera/Thinkstock; p. 7 Washington Post/Getty Images; p. 8 Bates Littlehales/National Geographic/Getty Images; pp. 9, 12, 16, 17, 19, 23 Jean-Erick Pasquier/Gamma-Rapho/Getty Images; p. 10 Sven-Erik Arndt/Picture Press/Getty Images; p. 14 Wyatt Rivard/Shutterstock.com; p. 15 NOAA photo library via Wikimedia Commons; p. 21 Christopher Furlong/Getty Images; p. 22 Sollina Images/The Image Bank/Getty Images; p. 27 Cavan Images/Iconica/Getty Images; p. 29 Jeremy Hardie/Photographer's Choice/Getty Images.

Printed in the United States of America

CPSIA compliance information: Batch #CS13GS: For further information contact Gareth Stevens, New York, New York at 1-800-542-2595.

CONTENTS

Words in the glossary appear in **bold** type the first time they are used in the text.

NOT A DAY AT THE BEACH

When you think of fishing, you might think of a fun day in a boat. When you're tired, you can go home to relax. But for a **commercial** fisherman, a normal day on the job isn't quite so enjoyable.

Fishermen may not come ashore for weeks—or even months. During that time, they work many hours each day. A fisherman stays on the job whether it's calm or stormy. Even on a beautiful day, commercial fishermen face the danger of a rogue wave overturning their boat! Fishermen face some of the most extreme conditions in their work, making their job one of the most dangerous in the world.

ROGUE WAVES

A rogue wave is a single wave of much greater height than the water around it, somewhat like a "wall of water." It can disappear as fast as it appears. Some scientists think these superwaves form when waves crash together. Rogue waves aren't reported very often but have been known to sink boats.

You know that fishing is exciting—and sometimes dangerous—when it captures national attention. Several popular TV shows highlight the adventures of commercial fishing crews.

5

SHOCKING NUMBERS

The US Bureau of Labor Statistics reported that fishermen are more likely to lose their lives on the job than police officers and security guards. To add to that, the National Institute for Occupational Safety and Health (NIOSH) reported that more than 500 fishermen died in the last 10 years.

But what's so dangerous about fishing? More than half these fishermen lost their lives after their boats flooded or were struck by bad weather. About one-third fell overboard. One-tenth were **injured** on the boat. All others were hurt diving or doing onshore jobs.

Fishing has been a way for people to get food for thousands of years. Today, as in the past, fishermen face the dangers of the open water.

7

FISHING IN ALASKA

As risky as commercial fishing is all over the world, Alaskan fishermen experience some of the greatest dangers. Almost half of the state's nongovernment jobs have to do with commercial fishing. That's more than 78,000 people. Sadly, about one-third of all on-the-job deaths in Alaska are fishing related.

Can you guess what the most dangerous kind of fishing in Alaska is? Pulling in a huge shark with a line? Nope! It's fishing for Alaskan king crab. Fishermen use huge, heavy traps called pots. They bait the pots, drop them into the ocean, and haul them in when they're full of crabs.

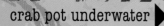
crab pot underwater ▶

Pots hold the crabs alive until the fishermen can haul in the catch.

SO WHY DO IT?

If it's so dangerous, why would people choose to be commercial fishermen? For one thing, money. US seafood industries earned over $13 billion in 2011. Some fishermen make a lot of money for a few days of work. And there's always a need for fish, to eat and to make various products.

King crab fishermen find their catch in areas of the Gulf of Alaska and the Bering Sea. The season for catching king crabs is between October and January and is often less than 4 weeks long. This may be the best time for catching crabs, but it's the worst time to be out on Alaskan waters!

These fishermen experience the coldest waters and weather conditions in the United States. Winter winds and ocean spray cause ice to build up all over the boat. Even dressed as warmly as possible, fishermen slide around on icy decks while moving pots that weigh hundreds of pounds.

FISHING SEASONS

Many states, including Alaska, require fishermen to have permits to fish. Even then, fishermen must follow rules about fishing seasons. Certain kinds of fish and **crustaceans** may not be caught during times of the year when they're mating or raising families. This is to protect fish and other sea creatures from dying out because of overfishing.

Overhead **equipment** on Alaskan fishing boats can collect ice. Fishermen need to watch their heads. If the sun comes out, the ice melts a bit and can fall on them.

Alaska is so far north that a winter day may have only a few hours of sunlight. This doesn't stop fishermen, though. Because the king crab season is short, fishermen work as long as 18 hours a day. Accidents can easily happen to tired crews working in the dark.

More than 80 percent of the deaths of Alaskan fishermen are due to drowning. Crew can slip on an ice-covered deck, get shoved by a big wave, or get knocked into the water by heavy equipment. Even if they're rescued from pitch-black waters, fishermen risk **hypothermia**.

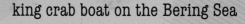
king crab boat on the Bering Sea

"WORST JOB WITH THE BEST PAY"

Businessweek magazine named crab fishing the "Worst Job with the Best Pay." Fishermen can make more than $40,000 for a few days of work if the haul is good—and even more if they're captains. That's why so many put up with such harsh conditions and terrible dangers.

13

THE BOAT

What does an Alaskan crab fishing boat look like? It needs to be big enough to carry everything a small crew needs for weeks out at sea. The boat is a place to work but also a minihome. It has beds, called bunks, and a kitchen, or scullery, with a stove, refrigerator, and other appliances.

Boats have many medical supplies since the crew can't get to a hospital quickly. Also, because of the high rate of drowning accidents, all fishing boats are required by law to have life rafts, survival suits, fire extinguishers, and equipment that can signal others if needed.

Some crab boats cost over $1 million because of their special equipment.

SURVIVAL SUITS

Survival suits aren't just life vests, although they do help people float. They provide protection against cold waters, too. They're big so that fishermen can put them on over their clothes. Each boat has one survival suit per crewmember in case the boat overturns, or capsizes.

practicing staying afloat in survival suits

A commercial fishing boat carries plenty of fishing equipment, including bait-cutting machines, **radar**, **sonar**, and GPS (global positioning systems).

A crab fishing boat may have as many as 300 steel crab pots on board. On average, a crab pot measures 7 feet by 7 feet by 3 feet (2.1 m by 2.1 m by 0.9 m). Each pot weighs about 700 pounds (318 kg). Boats have a crane and a **winch** to lower and raise them. A **buoy** marks each pot in the water so the crew knows where to retrieve it. The miles of rope needed to connect buoys and pots are also on board.

WINCH AND CRANE INJURIES

Crab pot winches and cranes commonly cause injuries. Pots may be dropped 400 feet (122 m) below the ocean's surface. Fishermen can get caught up in the long ropes. It can be hard to stop the machines fast enough to avoid injury.

Boats use sonar to locate crabs. However, sonar can miss crabs that are on or buried in the ocean floor. Sometimes captains just need to guess where to find them.

THROWING POTS

The ship's crane puts each pot onto a flat metal plate, or lift, attached to the side of the boat. First, a crewmember, called a deckhand, baits the pot. Then the lift tilts up, and the pot slides into the water. Crab pots are thrown out in a line over many miles. They sit, or "soak," for at least 24 hours.

When the boat comes back to retrieve a pot, the deckhand throws a hook to catch a rope attached to the buoy. The winch winds the rope and pulls the pot on board. The deckhands place it on the lift, open the pot, and **inspect** their haul.

KEEPERS

Not every king crab that walks into a pot is a "keeper." The crew can only keep adult male crabs. Crews aren't allowed to keep female crabs. This is so the females can help repopulate the ocean with king crabs. A crew that doesn't follow these rules may pay fines or lose their permit.

A crab pot has a funnel-like entrance. The crab crawls in to eat bait, such as herring and cod, but can't get back out.

19

THE CREW

While some fishing boats can have over 100 people on board, an Alaskan king crab boat may have fewer than 10 fishermen. Some crewmembers have certain jobs while others do a bit of everything.

The captain plans and oversees the whole operation, including where to fish, for how long, and how much to sell the haul for. The captain may provide the money needed to make the trip. Captains take a risk they won't make their money back.

Captains need to know how to steer the boat through bad weather and icy waters. Finally, they must be willing to put the crew's lives ahead of their own.

MARKET PRICE

The price of fish—and crabs—goes up and down. Sometimes, crews don't get as much money for a haul as they'd like. They may have an **auction** to sell to the highest bidder. They may also sell to **processors** who then sell to stores and restaurants. Other fishermen sell their haul at farmers' markets.

Some boats have first mates to take over when the captain is off duty.

Each ship needs an engineer to keep the boat's powerful engines and other equipment running well. This means working in an incredibly noisy engine room. Engineers wear special headphones to protect their hearing!

Ship engineers may maintain and operate the crane used to move pots around the deck. They take care of the onboard tanks that hold the live crabs after they're caught. They check for leaks in the boat and are ready to make repairs at any moment. Engineers must be able to think fast on little sleep. Besides all this, engineers help out with other tasks such as measuring crabs.

THE DERBY

King crab fishing boats have a maximum number, or quota, of crabs they can catch. Before 2005, boats fished for just a few days but were allowed to catch as many crabs as they wanted. This was called a derby. Authorities hope that conditions today are safer because crews stop working when they've caught the quota.

This crewmember guides a crab pot back onto the boat.

23

Deckhands do pretty much everything else on the boat. They must know how to tie knots, throw a hook, steer a ship, cook, and more. They load and unload equipment and supplies. Deckhands in Alaska need to do all these things in the dark and in freezing winds, too.

Even with a winch and crane, about three deckhands are needed to steady the heavy crab pots as they're lowered and raised. Each pot is worth about $1,000, so they have to be careful. In their spare time, they may use baseball bats to chip ice off the deck!

GREENHORNS

Greenhorns are deckhands who are new at the job. They often get the worst, most unpleasant tasks. However, it can be hard to get even a greenhorn's job. Captains usually don't want to hire new people who haven't proven their worth. Many greenhorns quit after their first trip.

Experienced deckhands are called boatswains or deck bosses. They watch over less skilled deckhands.

25

SAFETY MEASURES

Alaskan king crab boat captains have just days to bring in their quota. However, they and all captains need to follow certain safety measures to protect their crews. They should avoid fishing in bad conditions and make sure their boats are ready to withstand tough conditions. Between 2000 and 2010, 148 commercial fishing boats had **disasters** after experiencing floods, bad weather, and large waves.

NIOSH recommends that crews practice drills in case of disasters. They should also wear personal flotation devices anytime they're on deck. To avoid equipment accidents, alarms and automatic stopping devices can be put on winches in case deckhands get tangled in crab pot ropes.

MAN OVERBOARD

According to NIOSH, more than half of the fishermen who lost their lives by falling overboard between 2000 and 2010 were never even seen by their fellow fishermen. None were wearing survival suits, life vests, or other personal flotation devices. These might have saved their lives.

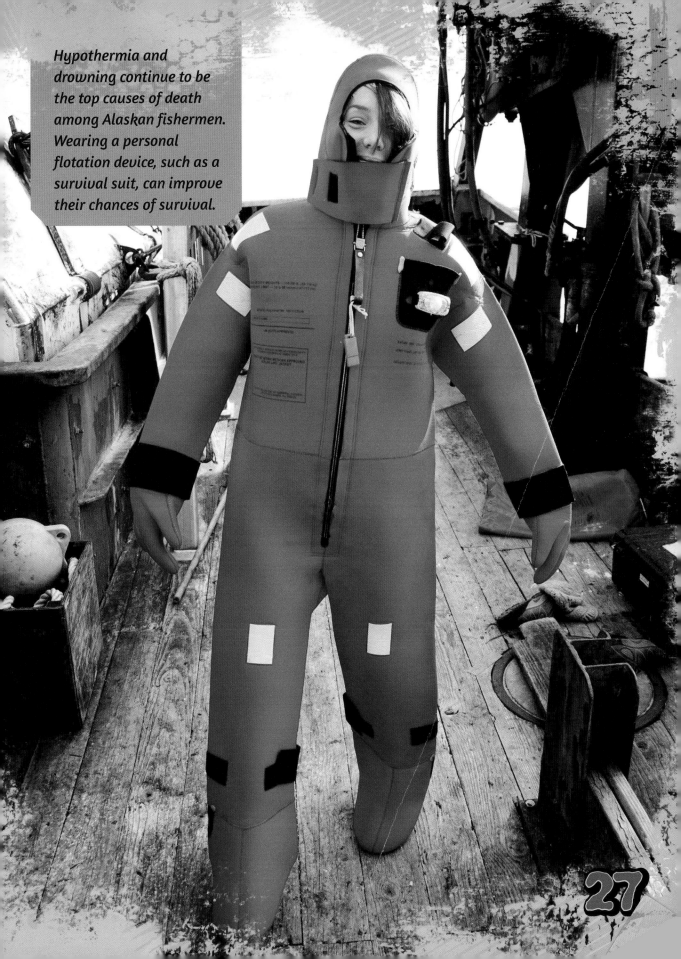

Hypothermia and drowning continue to be the top causes of death among Alaskan fishermen. Wearing a personal flotation device, such as a survival suit, can improve their chances of survival.

27

THE COAST GUARD STEPS IN

The US Coast Guard can inspect a commercial boat at any time to make sure it has its safety equipment. They can also keep a crew from fishing if they look unprepared or unskilled. These and other safety measures have decreased the number of deaths in Alaska during the last 20 years.

Sadly, states that don't have the same safety measures are still losing fishermen to accidents. Dungeness crab fishing crews in Oregon, Washington, and northern California now report more deaths than Alaskan crab fishermen. The boats there don't have quotas. Accidents happen because of overweight boats and untrained crews. Just a few safety measures can save lives.

THE COMPETITION

Because of the current king crab quota system, the numbers of boats and fishermen have shrunk. As many as 250 boats used to fish for crab in the Bering Sea. Now fewer than 125 do. Only about 500 fishermen are employed on these boats.